Illustrations by Richard Wright.
Book layout/design by Kathryn Edwards at kedwardscreative.com.

Visit us at www.motorheadgarageproductions.com

ISBN-13: 978-1717277961
ISBN-10: 1717277969

Dedicated To:

All the friends, family and followers who have
helped and supported me along the way.

And a very special thank you to my
designer Kathryn and my Illustrator Rich,
I can't thank you two enough.

Thank you.

T IS FOR TURBO
ABC BOOK

WRITTEN BY: MICHAEL J. MYERS
ILLUSTRATED BY: RICHARD A. WRIGHT

A IS FOR ALTERNATOR

THE ALTERNATOR CHARGES THE BATTERY.

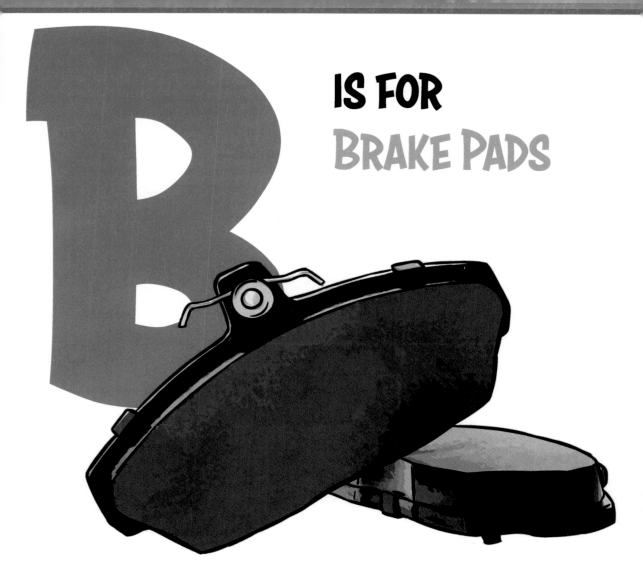

B

IS FOR
BRAKE PADS

THE BRAKE PADS SLOW THE CAR DOWN.

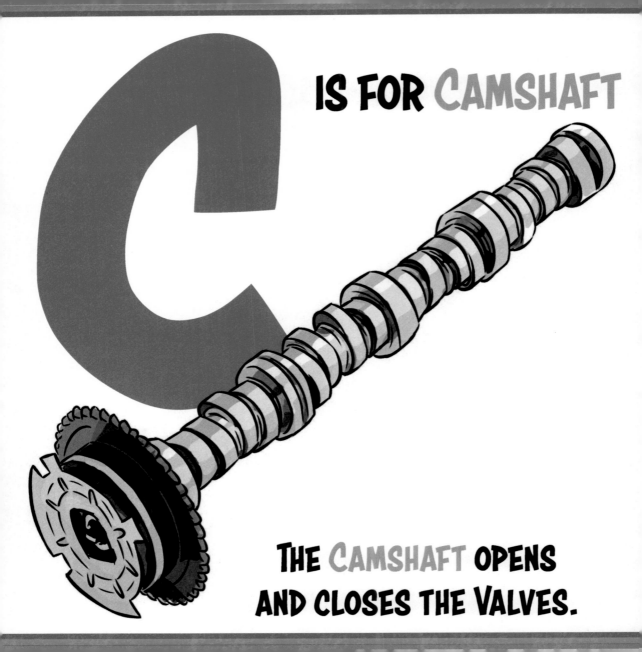

C IS FOR CAMSHAFT

THE CAMSHAFT OPENS AND CLOSES THE VALVES.

D IS FOR DIP-STICK

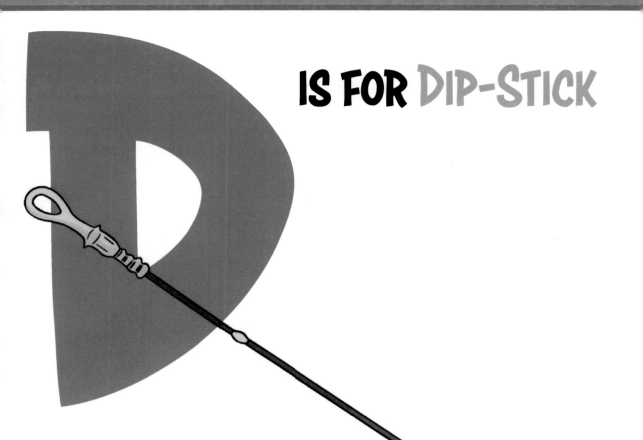

THE DIP-STICK CHECKS HOW MUCH OIL IS INSIDE THE ENGINE.

E

IS FOR
EXHAUST

THE EXHAUST RELEASES THE FUMES FROM THE ENGINE.

IS FOR FUEL TANK

THE FUEL TANK HOLDS THE CAR'S FUEL.

IS FOR GASKET

GASKETS HELP TO HOLD PRESSURE AND PREVENT LEAKS.

H
IS FOR HORN

HORNS GO BEEEEEP!

I IS FOR INTERCOOLER

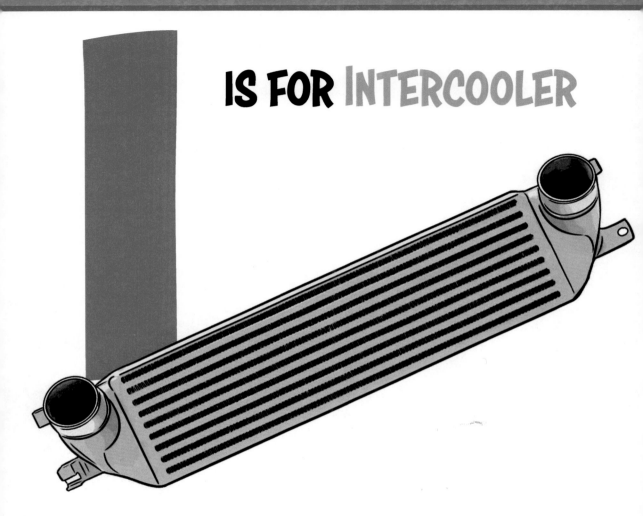

INTERCOOLERS COOL THE AIR
BEFORE IT GOES INTO THE TURBO.

IS FOR JACK-STAND

JACK-STANDS HOLD THE CAR UP IN THE AIR.

IS FOR KEYS

KEYS TURN THE CAR ON.

IS FOR LUG NUTS

LUG NUTS HOLD THE WHEELS ON.

M

IS FOR MANUAL TRANSMISSION

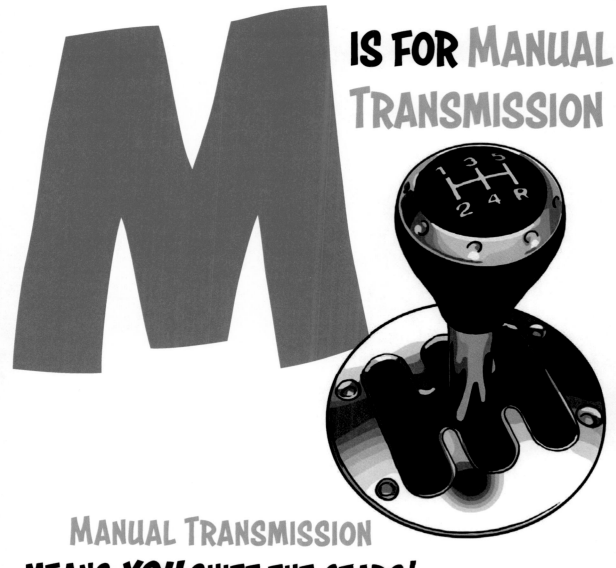

MANUAL TRANSMISSION
MEANS *YOU* SHIFT THE GEARS!

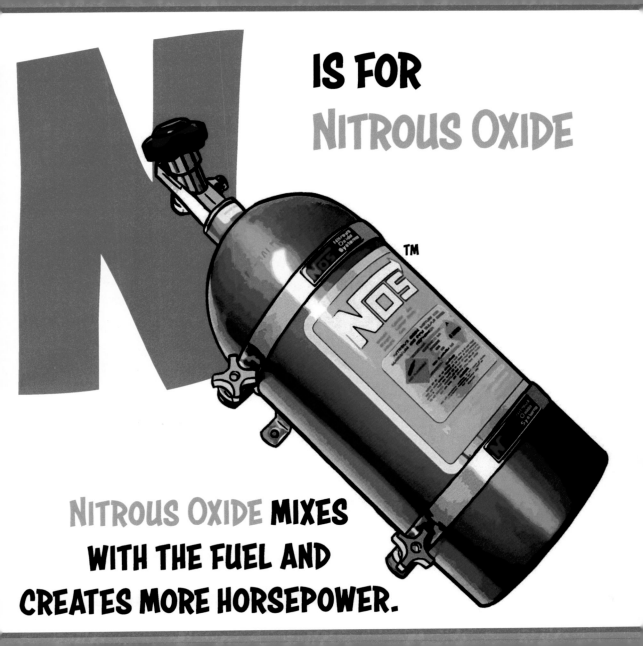

O IS FOR OIL FILTER

OIL FILTERS CLEAN THE OIL BEFORE IT CYCLES BACK THROUGH THE ENGINE.

IS FOR PISTONS

PISTONS MOVE UP AND DOWN INSIDE
THE ENGINE AND PRODUCE POWER!

IS FOR QUARTER MILE RACE

A QUARTER MILE RACE CAN LAST LESS THAN 10 SECONDS.

R IS FOR ROTOR

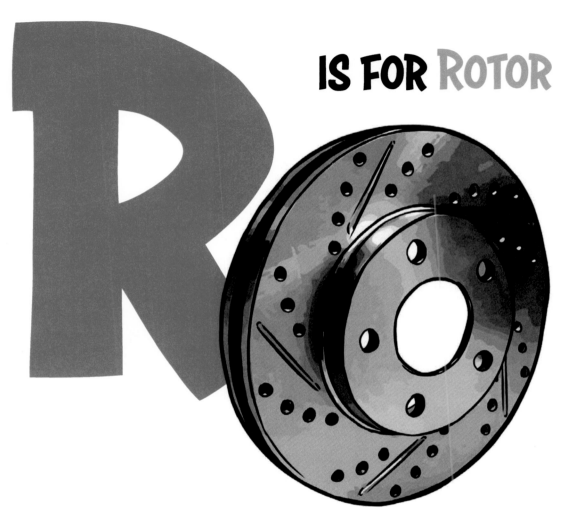

ROTORS ARE WHAT THE BRAKE PADS PRESS AGAINST TO SLOW THE CAR DOWN.

S

SUPERCHARGER

SUPERCHARGERS USE A BELT
TO FORCE AIR INTO THE ENGINE.

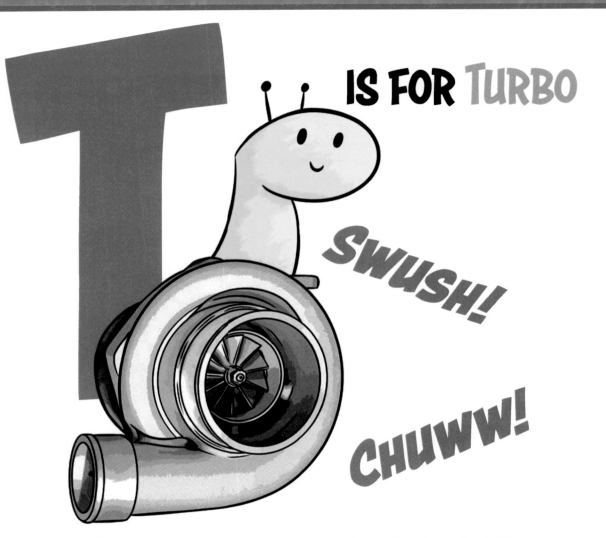

T IS FOR TURBO

SWUSH!

CHUWW!

TURBOCHARGERS ALSO FORCE AIR INTO THE MOTOR BY SPINNING A FAN.

IS FOR U-JOINT

U-JOINTS CONNECT TO THE DRIVESHAFT TO TRANSFER POWER FROM THE TRANSMISSION TO THE DIFFERENTIAL.

V IS FOR VALVE STEM

A VALVE STEM IS WHERE YOU PUT
THE AIR WHEN FILLING A TIRE.

W IS FOR WATER PUMP

THE WATER PUMP CYCLES COOLANT THROUGH THE ENGINE.

IS FOR XENON BULBS

XENON BULBS LIGHT UP BRIGHT!

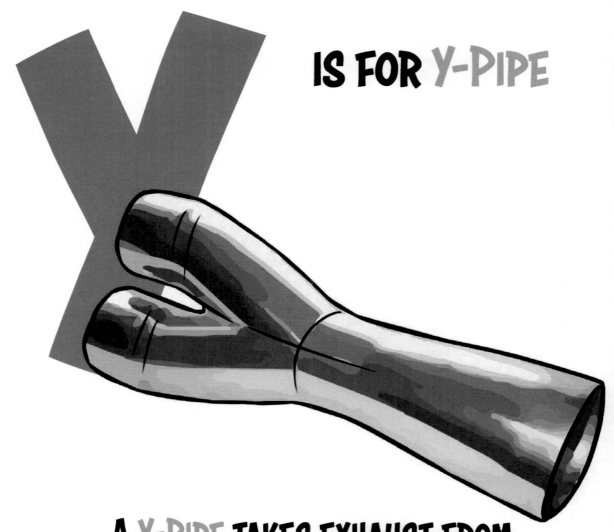

IS FOR Y-PIPE

A Y-PIPE TAKES EXHAUST FROM TWO PIPES AND FORCES IT INTO ONE.

Z IS FOR ZIP TIE

ZIP TIES CAN FIX ANYTHING.

Made in the USA
Lexington, KY
29 December 2018